MW00523204

Essential Question
How do inventions and technology
affect your life?

Ron's Radio

by Feana Tu'akoi
illustrated by Eric Scott Fisher

Chapter 1
Radio Dreaming 2

Chapter 2
The New Radio 5

Chapter 3
The Accident 9

Chapter 4
Uncle Joe to the Rescue 13

Respond to Reading 16

PAIRED READ Roosevelt's Fireside Chats . . 17

Focus on Genre 20

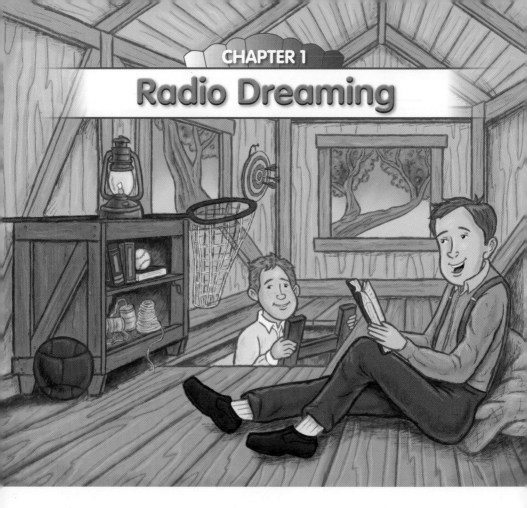

Radio Dreaming

"Guess what?" said Ron, as Jimmy climbed into the treehouse. "My family is getting a radio!"

"Is your Uncle Joe building you one?" Jimmy asked.

"No, but he'll be able to help Dad set it up," said Ron. "He's been working on **homemade** radios for more than a **decade**. Ever since he got back from the war."

Jimmy smiled. Ron was always talking about his uncle. Jimmy recited, "You told me that Uncle Joe builds his own radios. Once, he let you listen through the headphones, and you heard a **message** from a ship."

"But I'm not talking about a homemade radio now," Ron said excitedly. "This radio has the latest **technology**. We'll be able to listen to whatever we like."

Ron's father poked his head into the treehouse. "You boys won't be allowed to touch the radio. Remember what you did to my clock?"

The boys **squirmed** with **embarrassment**. When they were trying to figure out how the clock worked, they had pulled it apart. Then they couldn't put it back together.

"This radio is not a toy," Ron's dad said. "It's a wonder of modern **engineering**."

STOP AND CHECK

Why won't Ron's dad allow the boys to touch the new radio?

CHAPTER 2

The New Radio

When the radio finally arrived, Ron couldn't stop looking at it. It was tall and stood on the floor. It had a **gleaming** wooden cabinet. There was a speaker at the front so everyone could listen at the same time. Ron thought it was beautiful.

Uncle Joe and Ron's dad set up the radio in the living room. Uncle Joe turned the **dial**, or knob. He tuned in to a **station** to hear what was playing. There was a sh-sh-shh noise and then a blast of music.

"It looks easy to use," Ron's dad said. Ron thought so, too.

They moved the furniture around. Ron's mom **directed**, or showed, where to put everything. Now everyone could sit and listen to the radio together.

Uncle Joe gave the radio a final check. "You use this dial to find a station," he said.

"I can't wait to hear all the programs!" Ron said excitedly.

"You'll have to," said Ron's dad. "I don't want you going near the radio except when we listen to it together."

STOP AND CHECK

Why does Ron's family move the furniture?

CHAPTER 3

The Accident

Ron and his parents sat around the radio every evening. Ron sat quietly so his parents could hear every word.

Ron's parents listened to the news. They liked hearing about events in **faraway** places and different countries. The radio news was **current**, or up-to-date. They heard about things almost as soon as they happened.

Ron thought the news was boring, but he liked the programs about science and technology. He enjoyed listening to stories most of all.

One day, Jimmy came over. When Ron talked about the radio, Jimmy was **fascinated**. "Wow! Can I please see it?" he asked.

The boys **scouted** around to make sure Ron's parents were not around. Then they snuck into the living room.

Jimmy stared at the radio. "It's beautiful," he said.

Ron turned on the radio and moved the dial until he found a station.

The boys were listening to the radio when they heard the front gate open. They jumped up in a **panic**. Jimmy looked out the window. Ron's parents were home!

Jimmy cried, "Quick, turn it off!" He nudged Ron to hurry him up. Ron slipped and banged into the cabinet.

Everything went quiet. There was no sound from the radio.

Ron felt sick. "Go home, Jimmy. It's my fault. I'll figure out what to do."

STOP AND CHECK

What programs do Ron and his parents like to listen to on the radio?

CHAPTER 4

Uncle Joe to the Rescue

Ron told his parents about the radio when they came inside. They weren't angry, but they were sad and quiet. Ron felt terrible.

"Maybe Uncle Joe can fix it," he suggested.

Uncle Joe soon arrived. Everyone watched as he took the back off the radio and started **tinkering** with it.

"Ron, please go and get my toolbox," he said after a while.

Ron handed the toolbox to his uncle. Uncle Joe found a tool and used it to reattach a wire.

When Uncle Joe went around to the front of the cabinet, Ron held his breath and squeezed his eyes shut.

Suddenly, a voice sang out from the radio. Ron almost cried with relief.

Ron gave his uncle a huge hug. "Thank you, Uncle Joe! I promise I'll never touch the radio again!"

Then his father whispered something to Uncle Joe. Uncle Joe nodded and grinned.

"You can never touch this radio again, Ron," his dad said. "But I know you love listening to the radio, so you can have your own radio instead. Then you won't need to go near our radio."

He looked at Ron's mom, and she nodded.

"You'll need to earn the money to pay for the radio parts," Ron's dad said. "Then Uncle Joe will help you build it."

Ron was stunned. "Really?" he said.

Ron's mom grinned. "Ask Jimmy to help you. That should keep you both out of trouble!"

STOP AND CHECK

Why does Ron's father decide that Ron should build a radio of his own?

Respond to Reading

Summarize

Summarize how the radio affects Ron and his family. Your graphic organizer may help.

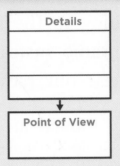

Details

↓

Point of View

Text Evidence

1. Is this story told by a first-person or a third-person narrator? Use examples from the text in your answer. POINT OF VIEW

2. Find the word *recited* on page 3. What does it mean? What clues in the text helped you figure out the meaning? VOCABULARY

3. Write about how the story would be different if Roy told it, as a first-person narrator. WRITE ABOUT READING

Compare Texts
Read about how President Roosevelt used
radio to talk to the American people.

Roosevelt's Fireside Chats

Franklin D. Roosevelt became President
of the United States in 1933. This was
during a hard time called the Great
Depression. Many banks, factories, and
stores closed. Millions of people lost their
jobs. President Roosevelt was worried about
the American people. He wanted to be
able to talk to them.

The Great Depression was
a difficult time for families.

President Roosevelt gave talks on the radio called "fireside chats." People listened to him in their living rooms. He often began his talks with "My friends."

President Roosevelt explained how the government was helping people. He also told listeners how they could help.

In the 1930s, people gathered to listen to the radio in the same way that they gather when they watch TV today. They listened to music, sports, comedy shows, and the news. People could hear news from around the world as it happened.

President Roosevelt did many fireside chats during the Depression. He asked people to keep using the banks. He asked them to support the government. The United States entered World War II in 1941. Roosevelt asked people to support the work that was being done for the war.

The talks were popular. They encouraged people during a difficult time in history.

President Roosevelt spoke to listeners as if he were a friend.

Make Connections

How did the radio make it possible for people to hear the latest news? ESSENTIAL QUESTION

Why was radio a good way for President Roosevelt to talk to people like Ron's parents? TEXT TO TEXT

Focus on Genre

Historical Fiction Historical fiction tells a story that is set in the past. It may be based on real facts. Historical fiction helps the reader understand life in the past.

Read and Find Historical fiction has details about the past. These give the reader information about the time when the story takes place. Details might be dates, events, clothing, or objects. How can you tell *Ron's Radio* is set in the past? Find details, such as the new radio.

Your Turn

Work with a partner. Talk about how you would use a radio if you lived in 1933. What would it look like? What would you listen to?

Imagine you lived in 1933. Draw a "photograph" of yourself and the inside of your house. Use details from the story to help you.